My
Ultimate
Softball
Journal

This Journal Belongs To:

_____

_____

Coach's Quote:

"Which is the most important play? The next one!"

Tracking my hits

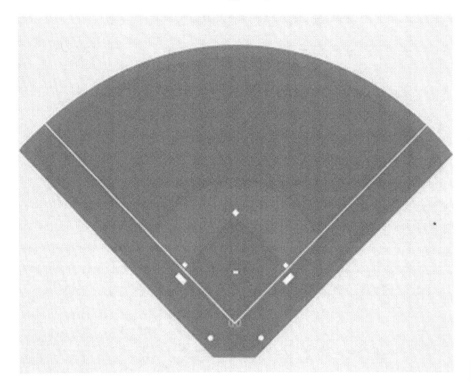

Opponent:

Game Date:

Where:

Positions Played:

Score:

Hitting:

Fielding Errors:

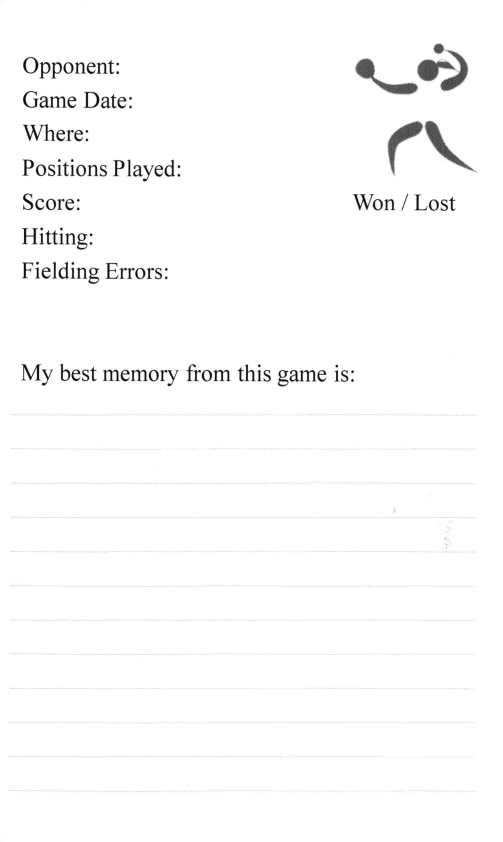

Won / Lost

My best memory from this game is:

Fan Feedback:

"It's just a game!"

Tracking my hits

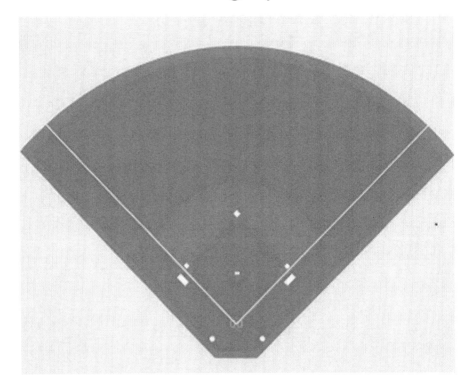

Opponent:

Game Date:

Where:

Positions Played:

Score:

Hitting:

Fielding Errors:

Won / Lost

My best memory from this game is:

Coach's Quote:

"Hard work pays off."

Tracking my hits

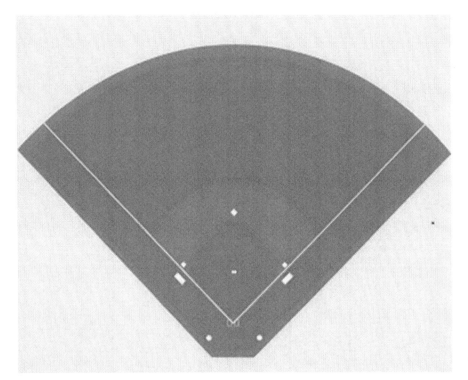

Opponent:

Game Date:

Where:

Positions Played:

Score:

Hitting:

Fielding Errors:

Won / Lost

My best memory from this game is:

Fan Feedback:

"Have fun!"

Tracking my hits

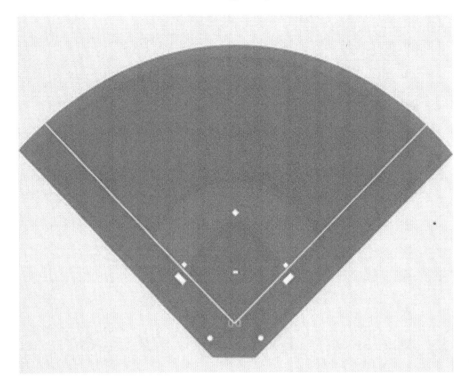

Opponent:

Game Date:

Where:

Positions Played:

Score:

Hitting:

Fielding Errors:

Won / Lost

My best memory from this game is:

Coach's Quote:

"Come on, you've gotta have those!"

Tracking my hits

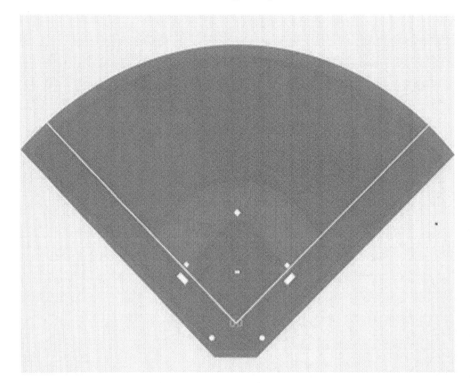

Opponent:

Game Date:

Where:

Positions Played:

Score: Won / Lost

Hitting:

Fielding Errors:

My best memory from this game is:

_____

_____

_____

_____

_____

_____

_____

_____

_____

Fan Feedback:

"Keep your eyes on the ball!"

Tracking my hits

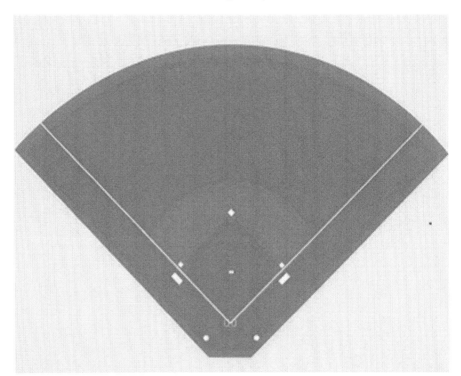

Opponent:

Game Date:

Where:

Positions Played:

Score:

Hitting:

Fielding Errors:

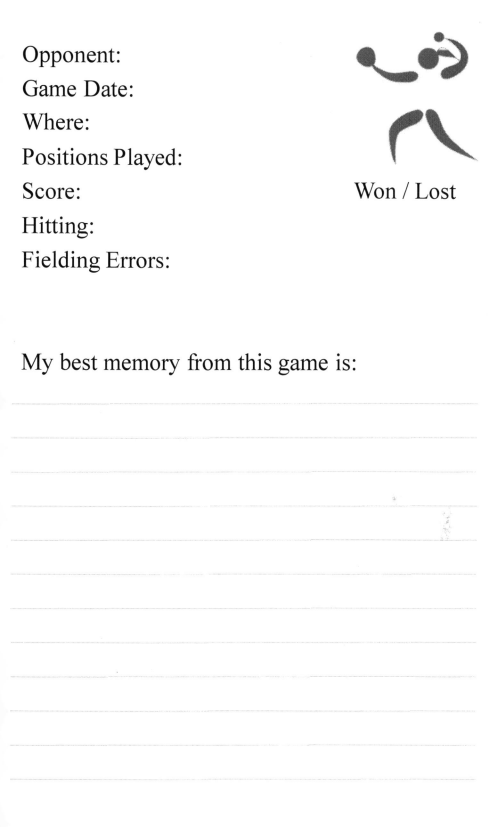

Won / Lost

My best memory from this game is:

_____

_____

_____

_____

_____

_____

_____

_____

_____

_____

Coach's Quote:

"Shake it off!"

Tracking my hits

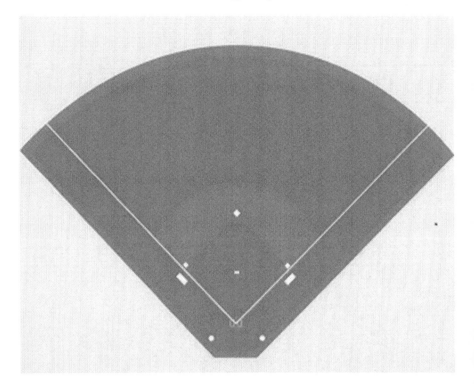

Opponent:

Game Date:

Where:

Positions Played:

Score: Won / Lost

Hitting:

Fielding Errors:

My best memory from this game is:

_____

_____

_____

_____

_____

_____

_____

_____

_____

Fan Feedback:

"Watch the change-up!"

Tracking my hits

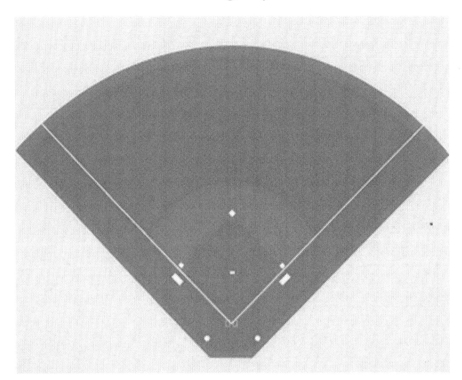

Opponent:

Game Date:

Where:

Positions Played:

Score: Won / Lost

Hitting:

Fielding Errors:

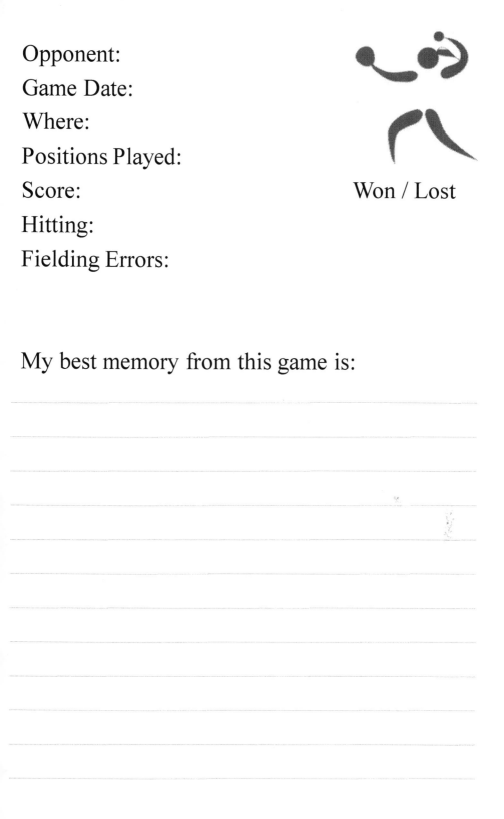

My best memory from this game is:

Coach's Quote:

"Somebody make a play!"

Tracking my hits

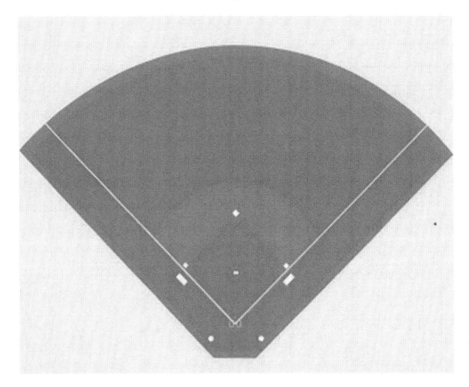

Opponent:

Game Date:

Where:

Positions Played:

Score: Won / Lost

Hitting:

Fielding Errors:

My best memory from this game is:

_____

_____

_____

_____

_____

_____

_____

_____

Fan Feedback:

"Expect it!"

Tracking my hits

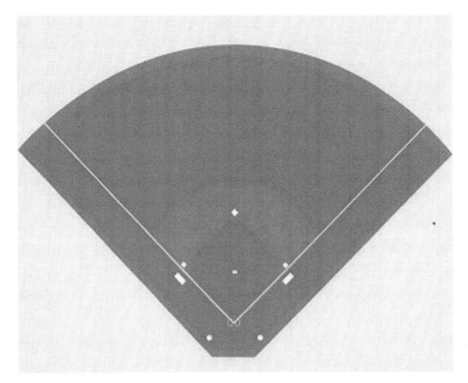

Opponent:

Game Date:

Where:

Positions Played:

Score: Won / Lost

Hitting:

Fielding Errors:

My best memory from this game is:

Coach's Quote:

"Know your count!"

Tracking my hits

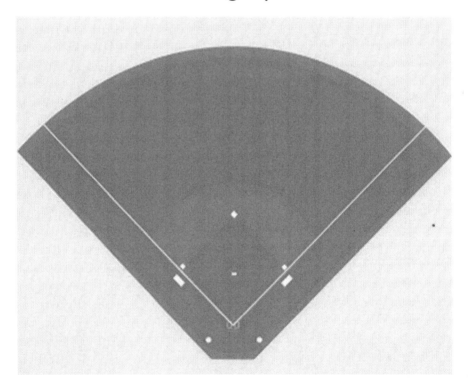

Opponent:

Game Date:

Where:

Positions Played:

Score: Won / Lost

Hitting:

Fielding Errors:

My best memory from this game is:

Fan Feedback:

"Did you get a picture of that play?"

Tracking my hits

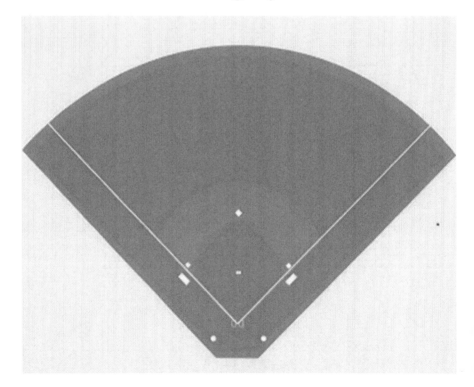

Opponent:

Game Date:

Where:

Positions Played:

Score: Won / Lost

Hitting:

Fielding Errors:

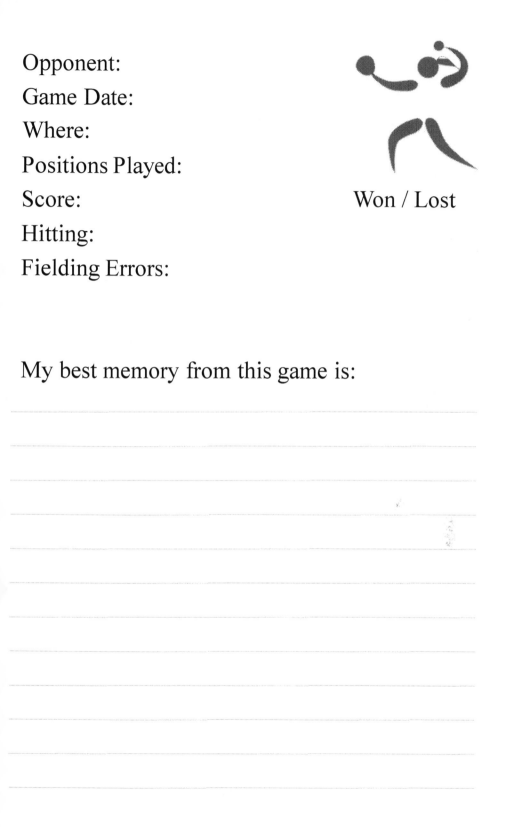

My best memory from this game is:

Coach's Quote:

"Get your bat and time her!"

Tracking my hits

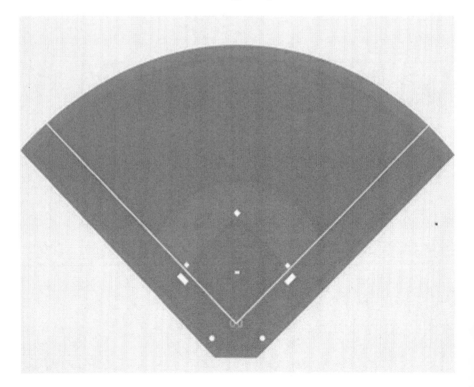

Opponent:

Game Date:

Where:

Positions Played:

Score: Won / Lost

Hitting:

Fielding Errors:

My best memory from this game is:

_____

_____

_____

_____

_____

_____

_____

_____

_____

Fan Feedback:

"Wait on it!"

Tracking my hits

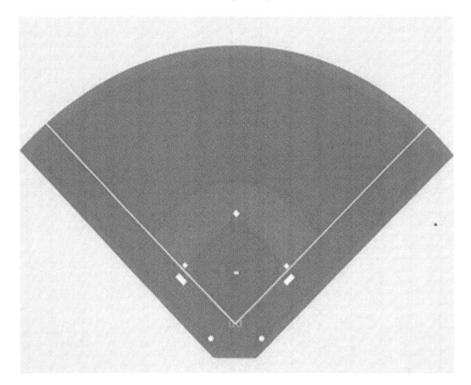

Opponent:

Game Date:

Where:

Positions Played:

Score:

Hitting:

Fielding Errors:

Won / Lost

My best memory from this game is:

Coach's Quote:

"New PITCHER!"

Tracking my hits

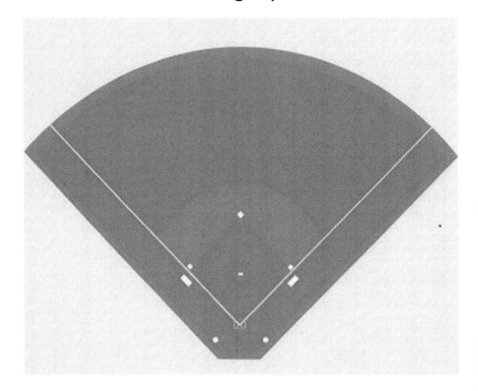

Opponent:

Game Date:

Where:

Positions Played:

Score: Won / Lost

Hitting:

Fielding Errors:

My best memory from this game is:

_____

_____

_____

_____

_____

_____

_____

_____

Fan Feedback:

"Field it clean!"

Tracking my hits

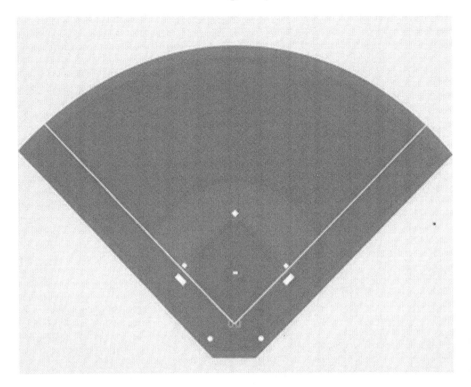

Opponent:

Game Date:

Where:

Positions Played:

Score: Won / Lost

Hitting:

Fielding Errors:

My best memory from this game is:

_____

_____

_____

_____

_____

_____

_____

_____

_____

Coach's Quote:

"I can tell who's practicing at home."

Tracking my hits

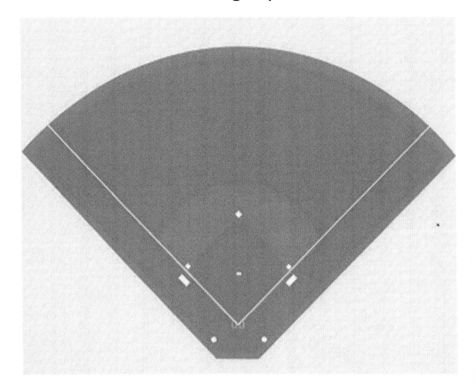

Opponent:

Game Date:

Where:

Positions Played:

Score: Won / Lost

Hitting:

Fielding Errors:

My best memory from this game is:

Fan Feedback:

"Talk to each other!"

Tracking my hits

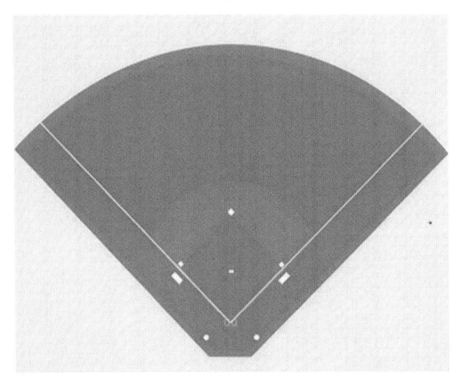

Opponent:

Game Date:

Where:

Positions Played:

Score:

Won / Lost

Hitting:

Fielding Errors:

My best memory from this game is:

Coach's Quote:

"Go two, Go TWO!"

Tracking my hits

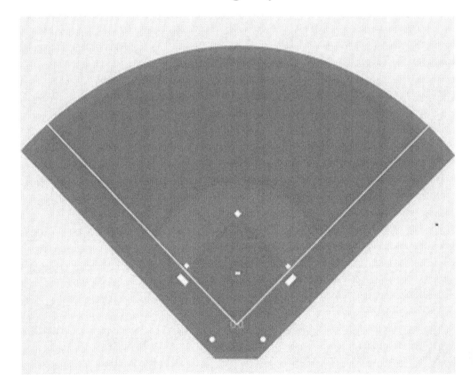

Opponent:

Game Date:

Where:

Positions Played:

Score: Won / Lost

Hitting:

Fielding Errors:

My best memory from this game is:

_____

_____

_____

_____

_____

_____

_____

_____

_____

_____

Fan Feedback:

"Somebody get an out!"

Tracking my hits

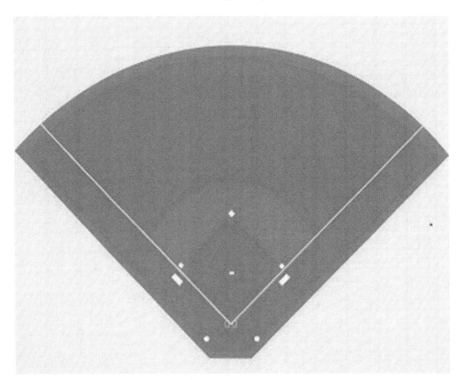

Opponent:

Game Date:

Where:

Positions Played:

Score: Won / Lost

Hitting:

Fielding Errors:

My best memory from this game is:

Coach's Quote:

"You've got to hit your cutoff!"

Tracking my hits

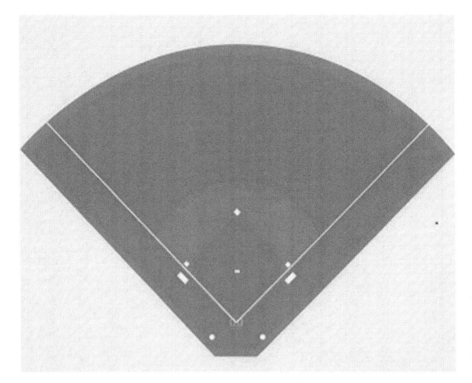

Opponent:

Game Date:

Where:

Positions Played:

Score: Won / Lost

Hitting:

Fielding Errors:

My best memory from this game is:

_____

_____

_____

_____

_____

_____

_____

_____

_____

Fan Feedback:

"Don't help her out!"

Tracking my hits

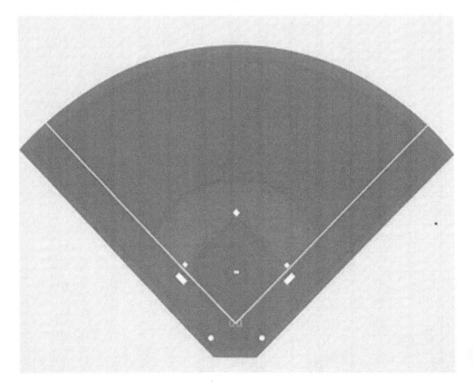

Opponent:

Game Date:

Where:

Positions Played:

Score: Won / Lost

Hitting:

Fielding Errors:

My best memory from this game is:

_____

_____

_____

_____

_____

_____

_____

_____

Coach's Quote:

"I can't want it for you."

Tracking my hits

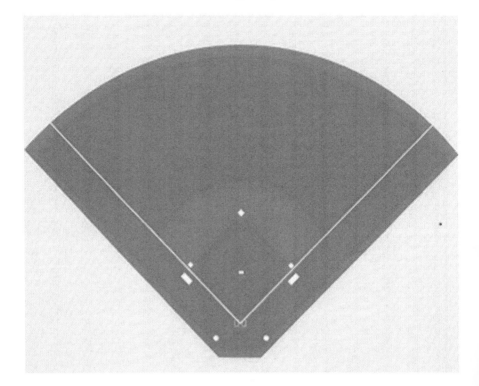

Opponent:

Game Date:

Where:

Positions Played:

Score: Won / Lost

Hitting:

Fielding Errors:

My best memory from this game is:

_____

_____

_____

_____

_____

_____

_____

_____

_____

Fan Feedback:

"You're way ahead!"

Tracking my hits

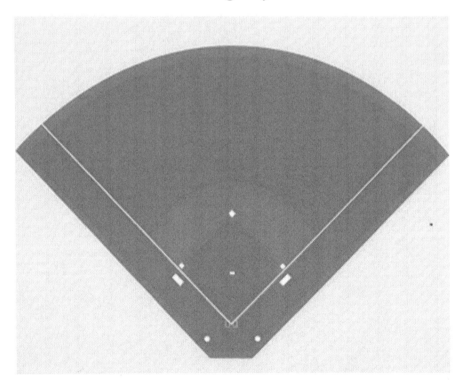

Opponent:

Game Date:

Where:

Positions Played:

Score: Won / Lost

Hitting:

Fielding Errors:

My best memory from this game is:

_____

_____

_____

_____

_____

_____

_____

_____

_____

Coach's Quote:

"Don't watch a third strike!"

Tracking my hits

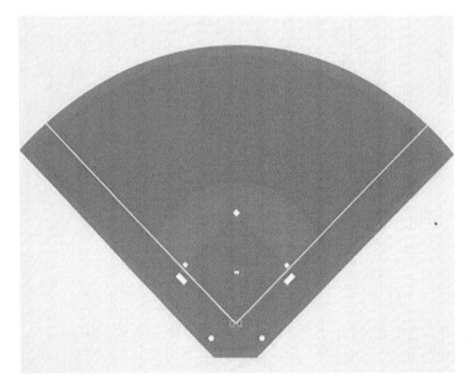

Opponent:

Game Date:

Where:

Positions Played:

Score: Won / Lost

Hitting:

Fielding Errors:

My best memory from this game is:

_____

_____

_____

_____

_____

_____

_____

_____

_____

_____

Fan Feedback:

"Good take!"

Tracking my hits

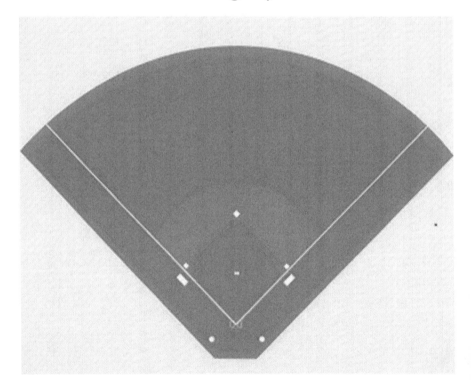

Opponent:

Game Date:

Where:

Positions Played:

Score: Won / Lost

Hitting:

Fielding Errors:

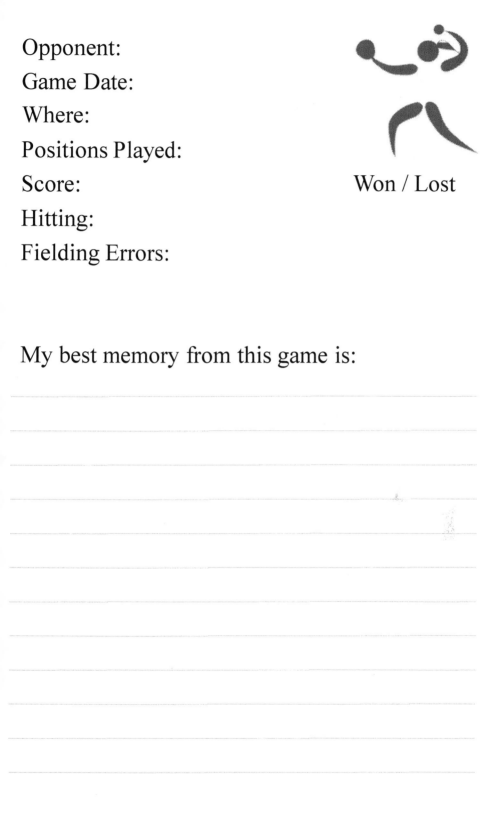

My best memory from this game is:

_____

_____

_____

_____

_____

_____

_____

_____

Coach's Quote:

"Be aggressive!"

Tracking my hits

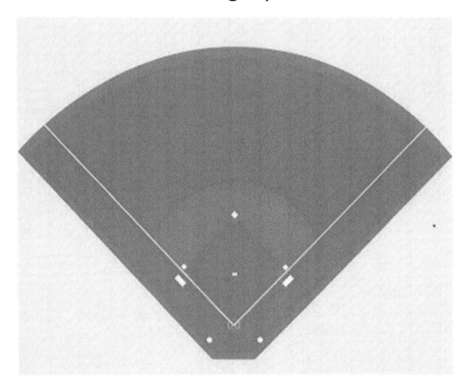

Opponent:

Game Date:

Where:

Positions Played:

Score: Won / Lost

Hitting:

Fielding Errors:

My best memory from this game is:

_____

_____

_____

_____

_____

_____

_____

_____

Fan Feedback:

"Not your pitch!"

Tracking my hits

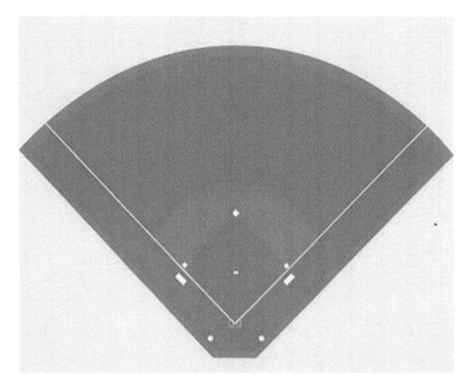

Opponent:

Game Date:

Where:

Positions Played:

Score: Won / Lost

Hitting:

Fielding Errors:

My best memory from this game is:

Coach's Quote:

"Lay off the junk!"

Tracking my hits

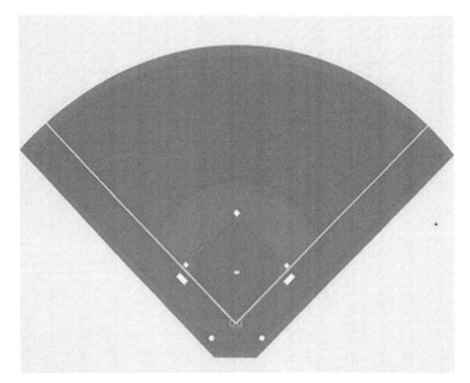

Opponent:

Game Date:

Where:

Positions Played:

Score: Won / Lost

Hitting:

Fielding Errors:

My best memory from this game is:

_____

_____

_____

_____

_____

_____

_____

_____

_____

_____

Fan Feedback:

"Watch the ball hit your bat!"

Tracking my hits

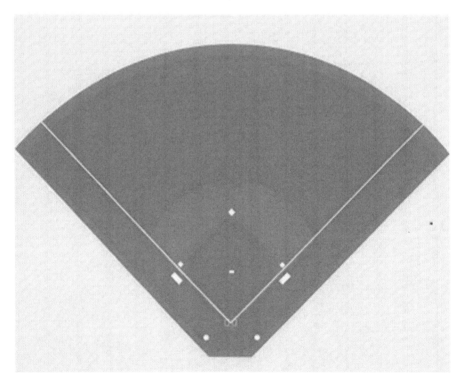

Opponent:

Game Date:

Where:

Positions Played:

Score: Won / Lost

Hitting:

Fielding Errors:

My best memory from this game is:

_____

_____

_____

_____

_____

_____

_____

_____

_____

_____

Coach's Quote:

"Let's get the bats going!"

Tracking my hits

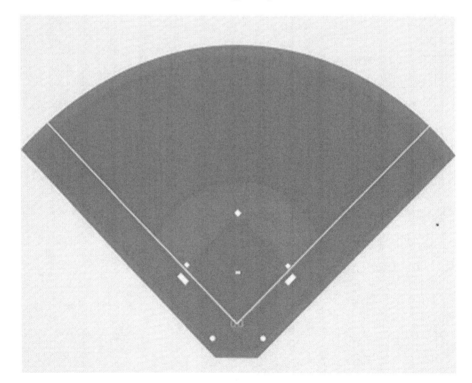

Opponent:

Game Date:

Where:

Positions Played:

Score: Won / Lost

Hitting:

Fielding Errors:

My best memory from this game is:

Fan Feedback:

"Get dirty!"

Tracking my hits

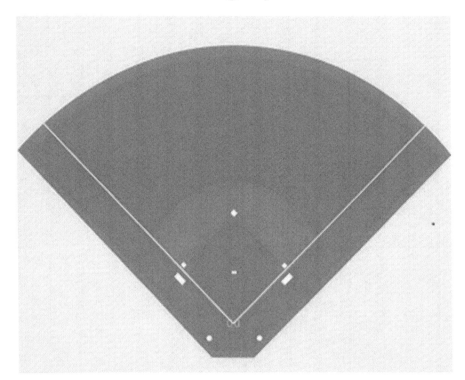

Opponent:

Game Date:

Where:

Positions Played:

Score:

Hitting:

Fielding Errors:

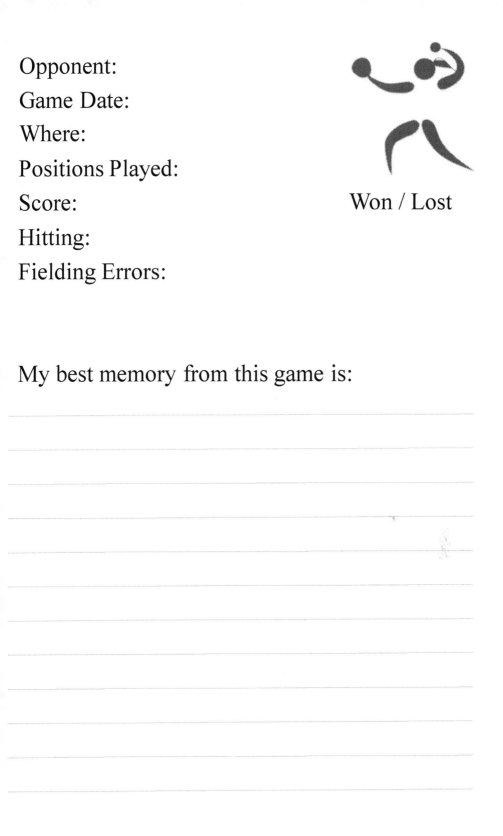

Won / Lost

My best memory from this game is:

Coach's Quote:

"Great play!"

Tracking my hits

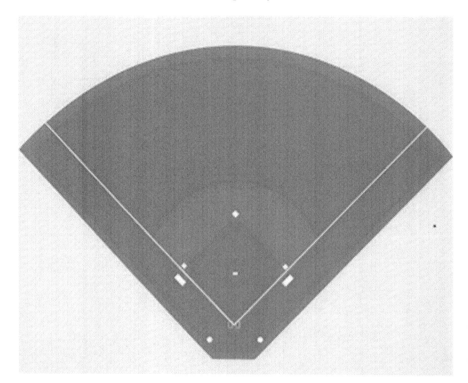

Opponent:

Game Date:

Where:

Positions Played:

Score:

Hitting:

Fielding Errors:

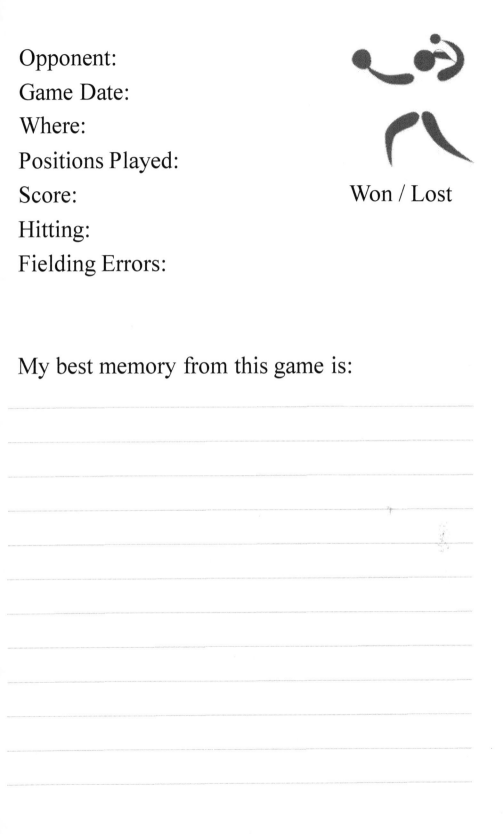

Won / Lost

My best memory from this game is:

Fan Feedback:

"Ready position!"

Tracking my hits

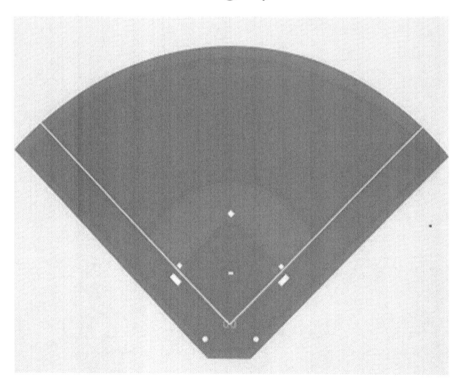

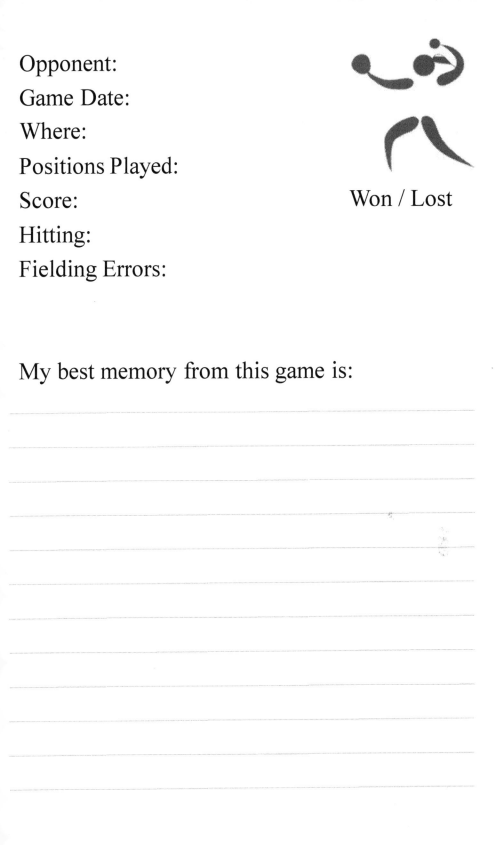

Opponent:

Game Date:

Where:

Positions Played:

Score: Won / Lost

Hitting:

Fielding Errors:

My best memory from this game is:

Coach's Quote:

"I'll deal with the umpires."

Tracking my hits

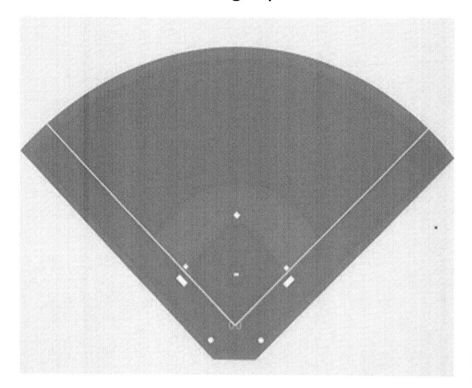

Opponent:

Game Date:

Where:

Positions Played:

Score:

Hitting:

Fielding Errors:

Won / Lost

My best memory from this game is:

Fan Feedback:

"Roll it up!"

Tracking my hits

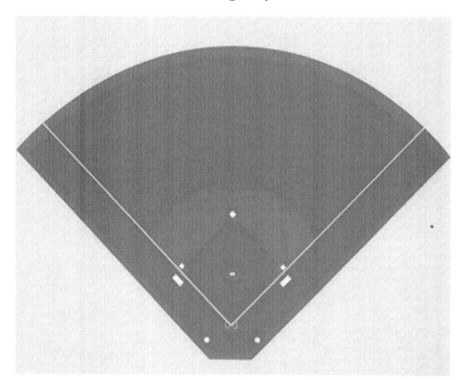

Opponent:

Game Date:

Where:

Positions Played:

Score:

Hitting:

Fielding Errors:

Won / Lost

My best memory from this game is:

Coach's Quote:

"Don't walk on my field!"

Tracking my hits

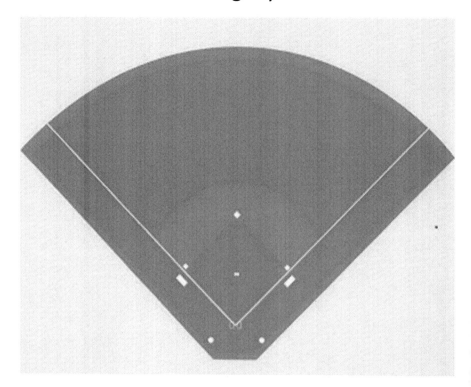

Opponent:

Game Date:

Where:

Positions Played:

Score:

Hitting:

Fielding Errors:

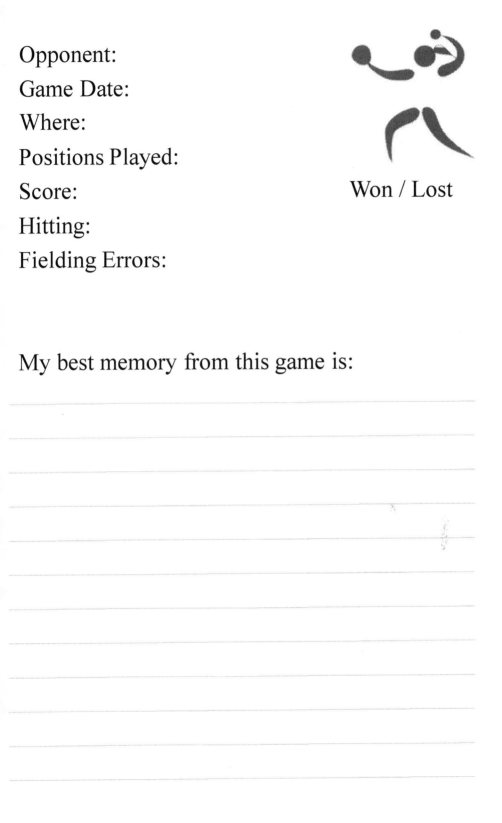

Won / Lost

My best memory from this game is:

Fan Feedback:

"Who's idea was it to get white pants?"

Tracking my hits

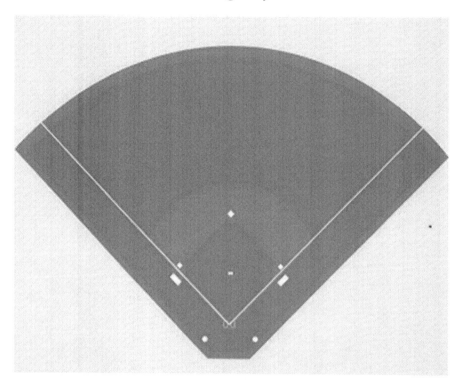

Opponent:

Game Date:

Where:

Positions Played:

Score:

Hitting:

Fielding Errors:

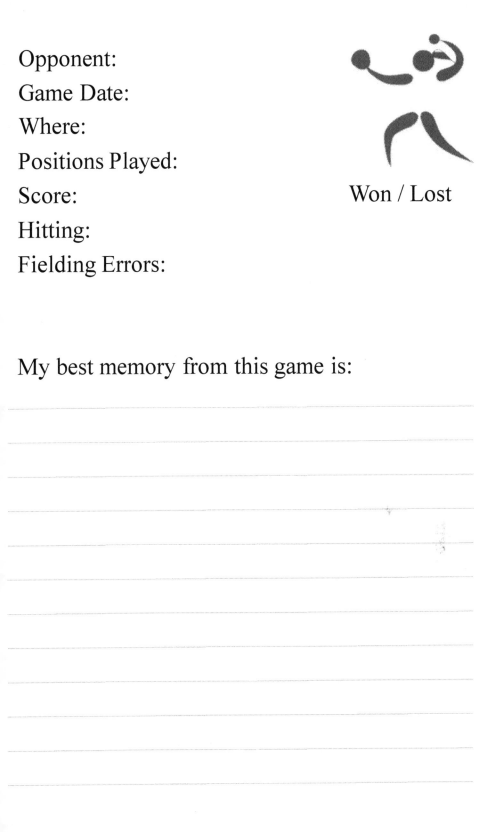

Won / Lost

My best memory from this game is:

Coach's Quote:

"Have a plan!

Tracking my hits

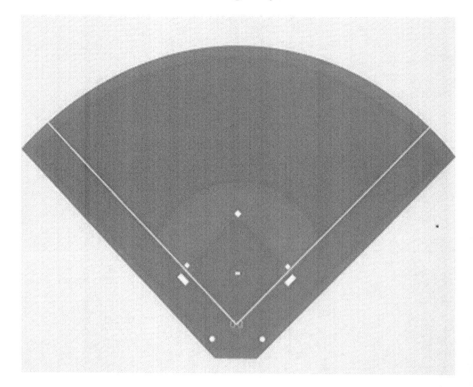

Opponent:

Game Date:

Where:

Positions Played:

Score:

Won / Lost

Hitting:

Fielding Errors:

My best memory from this game is:

Fan Feedback:

"Win this game and you can sleep later tomorrow!"

Tracking my hits

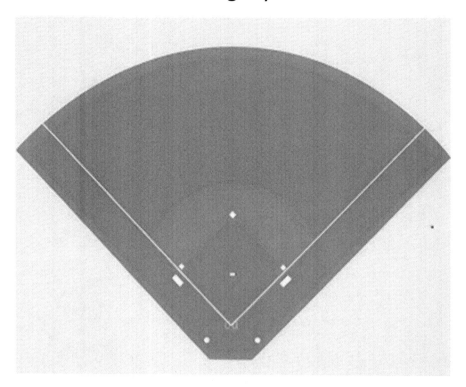

Opponent:

Game Date:

Where:

Positions Played:

Score: Won / Lost

Hitting:

Fielding Errors:

My best memory from this game is:

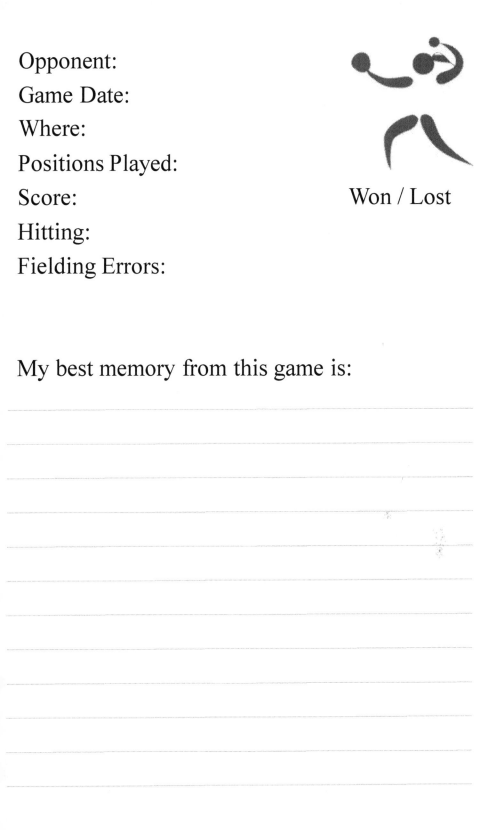

Coach's Quote:

"Know the situation!"

Tracking my hits

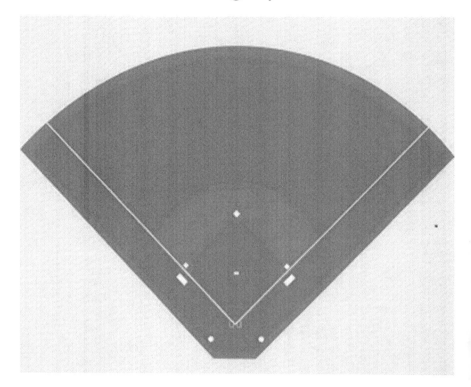

Opponent:

Game Date:

Where:

Positions Played:

Score:

Hitting:

Fielding Errors:

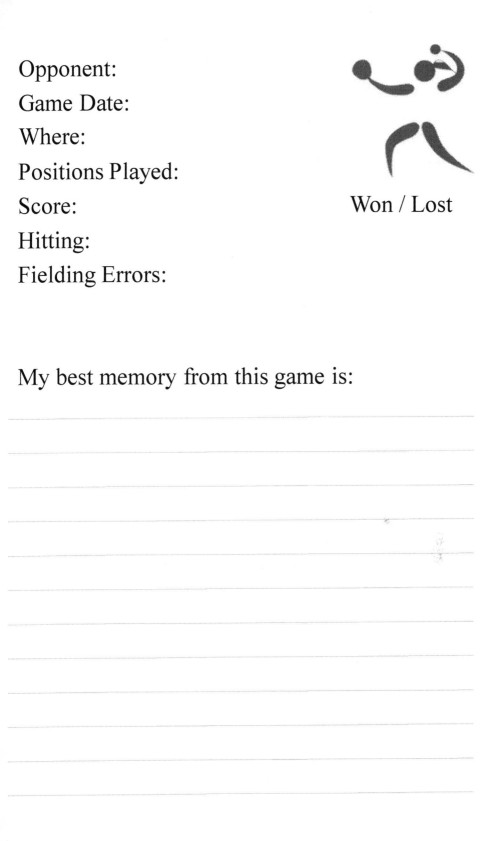

Won / Lost

My best memory from this game is:

Fan Feedback:

"HEADS UP!"

Tracking my hits

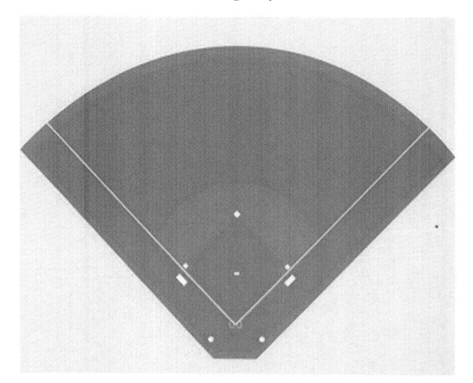

Opponent:

Game Date:

Where:

Positions Played:

Score:

Won / Lost

Hitting:

Fielding Errors:

My best memory from this game is:

_____

_____

_____

_____

_____

_____

_____

_____

_____

_____

Coach's Quote:

"Give her a look back, then go ONE.

Tracking my hits

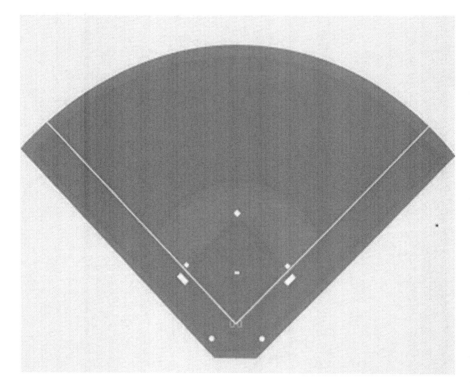

Opponent:

Game Date:

Where:

Positions Played:

Score:

Hitting:

Fielding Errors:

Won / Lost

My best memory from this game is:

Fan Feedback:

"That gate fee is ridiculous!"

Tracking my hits

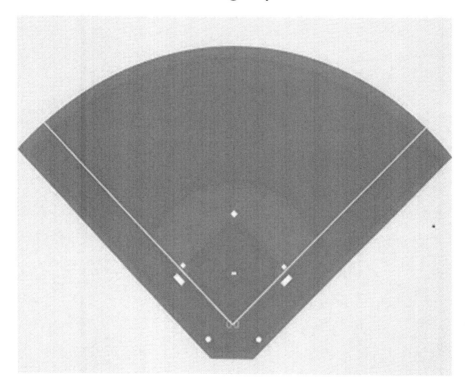

Opponent:

Game Date:

Where:

Positions Played:

Score:

Hitting:

Fielding Errors:

Won / Lost

My best memory from this game is:

_____

_____

_____

_____

_____

_____

_____

_____

Coach's Quote:

"Did someone get that foul ball?"

Tracking my hits

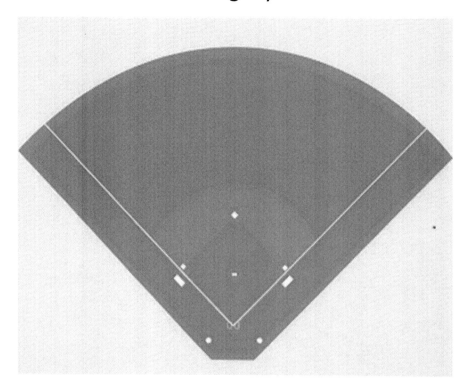

Opponent:

Game Date:

Where:

Positions Played:

Score:

Hitting:

Fielding Errors:

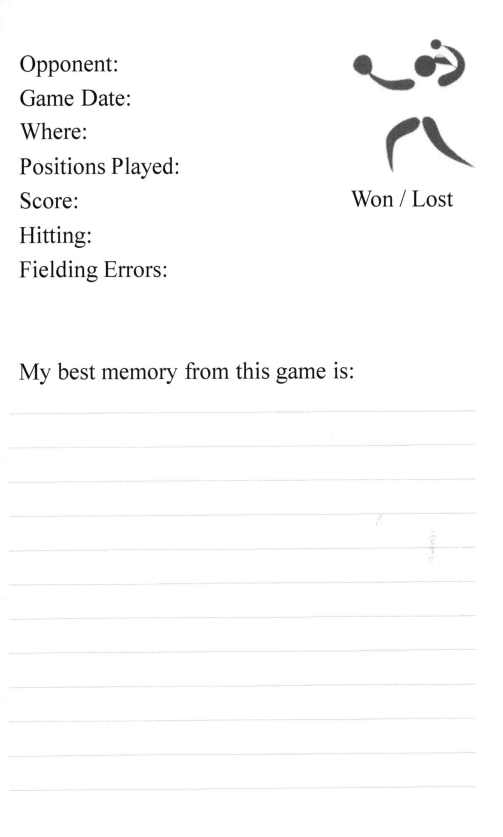

Won / Lost

My best memory from this game is:

Fan Feedback:

"Don't tell <u>me</u> I can't bring in my cooler!"

Tracking my hits

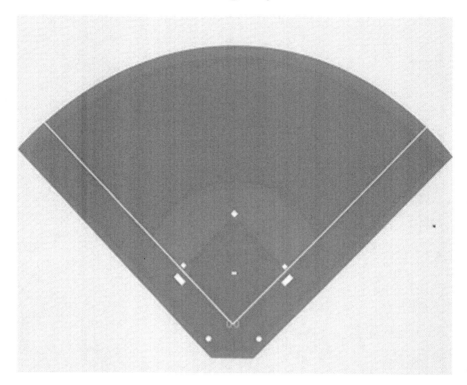

Opponent:

Game Date:

Where:

Positions Played:

Score:

Hitting:

Fielding Errors:

Won / Lost

My best memory from this game is:

Coach's Quote:

"You've gotta finish your pitch!"

Tracking my hits

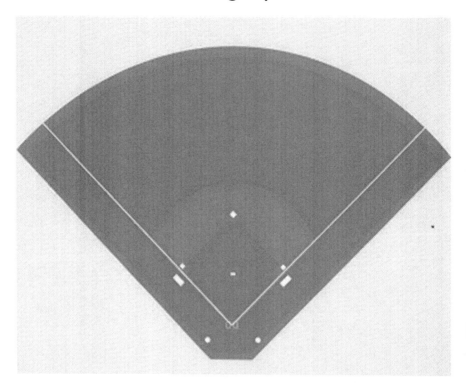

Opponent:

Game Date:

Where:

Positions Played:

Score:

Won / Lost

Hitting:

Fielding Errors:

My best memory from this game is:

_____

_____

_____

_____

_____

_____

_____

_____

_____

_____

_____

Fan Feedback:

"Make sure you're drinking enough water!"

Tracking my hits

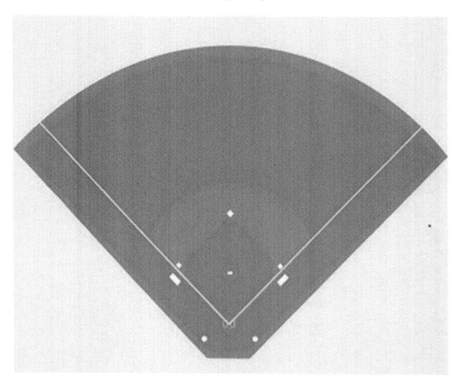

Opponent:

Game Date:

Where:

Positions Played:

Score:

Hitting:

Fielding Errors:

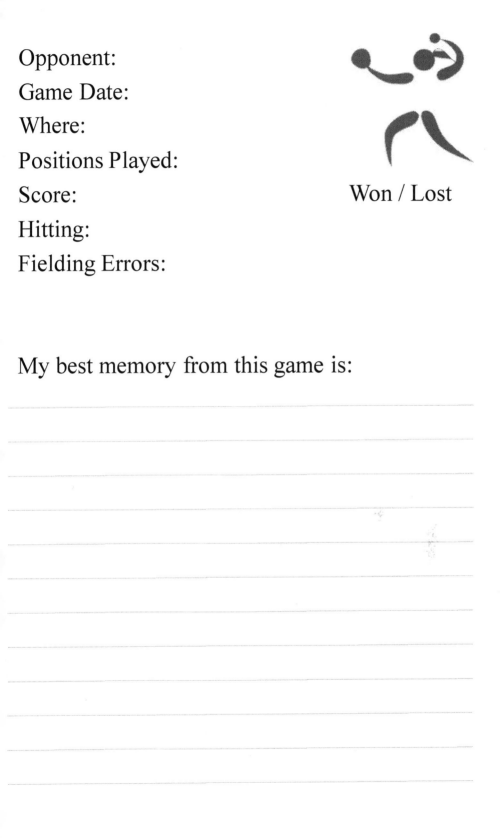

Won / Lost

My best memory from this game is:

Coach's Quote:

"Make it a quick half!"

Tracking my hits

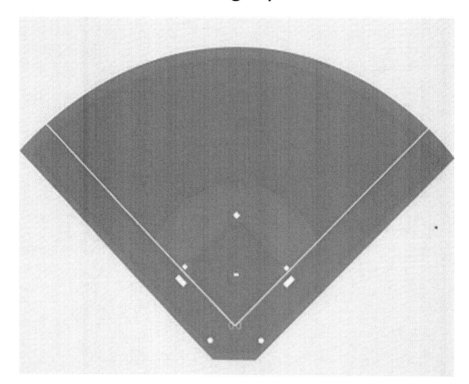

Opponent:

Game Date:

Where:

Positions Played:

Score:

Hitting:

Fielding Errors:

Won / Lost

My best memory from this game is:

Fan Feedback:

"Is all your stuff in your bag?"

Tracking my hits

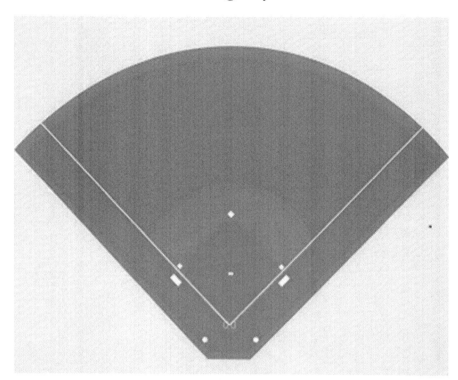

Opponent:

Game Date:

Where:

Positions Played:

Score:

Won / Lost

Hitting:

Fielding Errors:

My best memory from this game is:

_____

_____

_____

_____

_____

_____

_____

_____

_____

Coach's Quote:

"Leave it all on the field!"

Tracking my hits

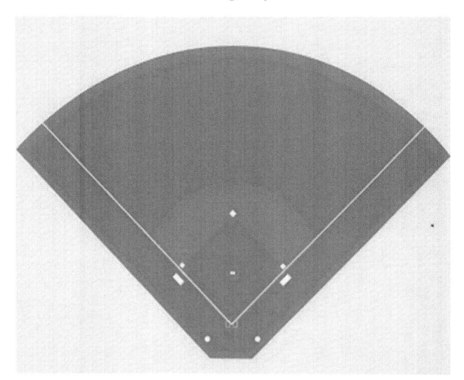

Opponent:

Game Date:

Where:

Positions Played:

Score:

Hitting:

Fielding Errors:

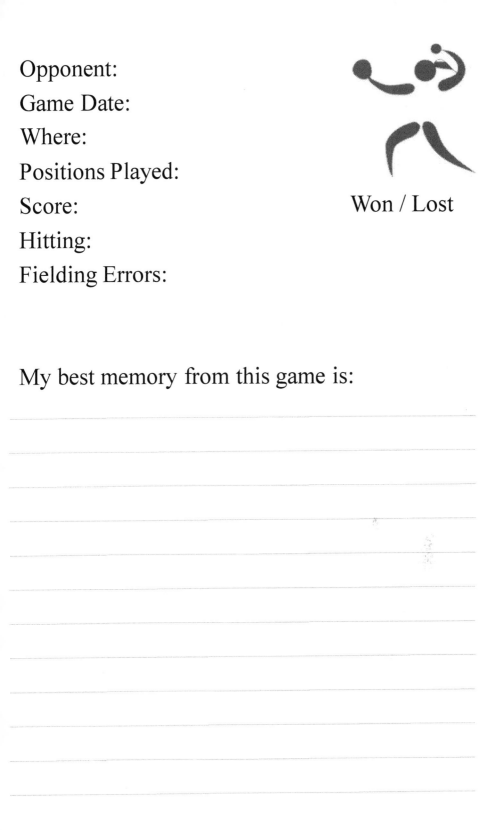

Won / Lost

My best memory from this game is:

Fan Feedback:

"Hey, leave those up there!"

Tracking my hits

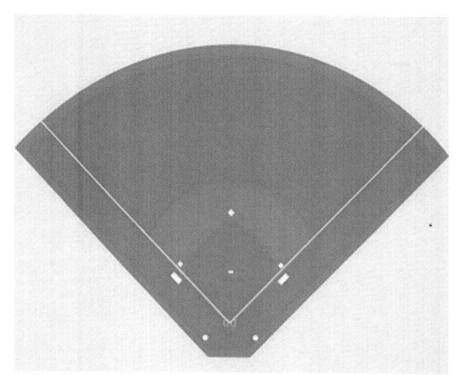

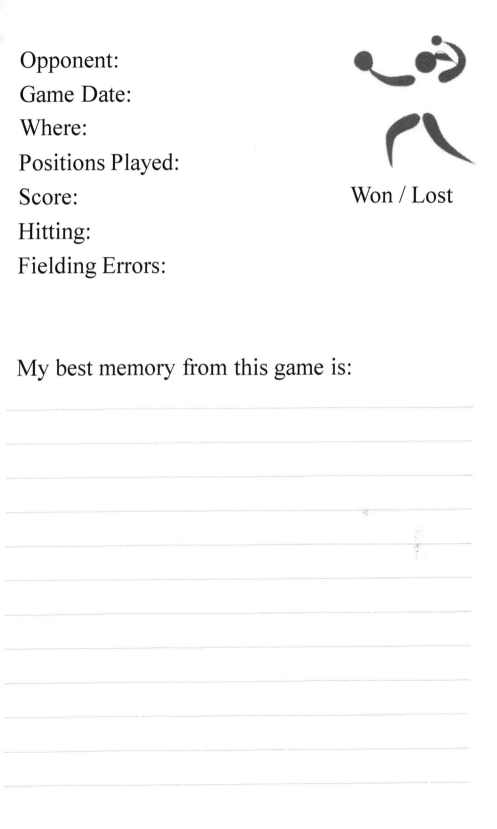

Opponent:

Game Date:

Where:

Positions Played:

Score:

Hitting:

Fielding Errors:

Won / Lost

My best memory from this game is:

Coach's Quote:

"Don't rub it!"

Tracking my hits

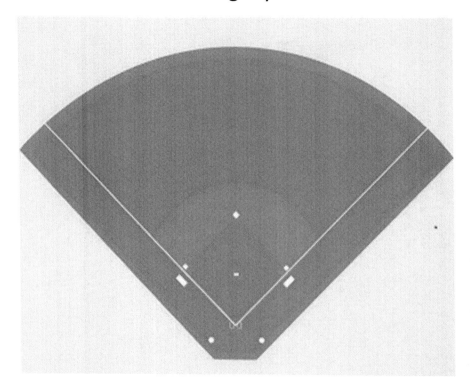

Opponent:

Game Date:

Where:

Positions Played:

Score:

Hitting:

Fielding Errors:

Won / Lost

My best memory from this game is:

Fan Feedback:

"We're not playing golf!"

Tracking my hits

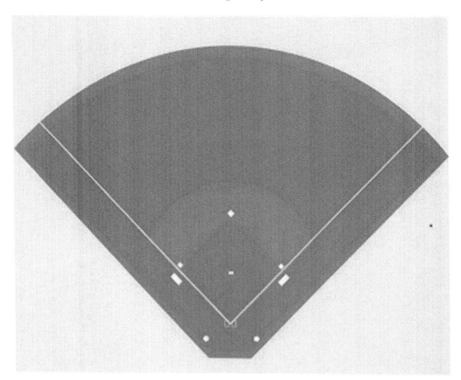

Opponent:

Game Date:

Where:

Positions Played:

Score:

Hitting:

Fielding Errors:

Won / Lost

My best memory from this game is:

Coach's Quote:

"What was THAT?"

Tracking my hits

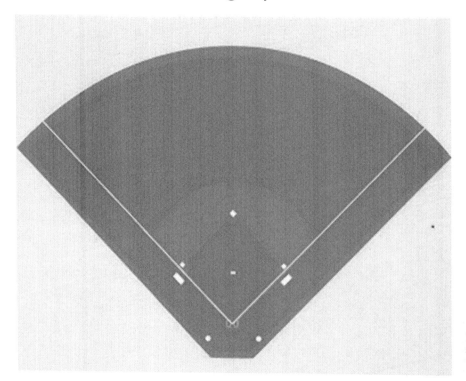

Opponent:

Game Date:

Where:

Positions Played:

Score:

Hitting:

Fielding Errors:

Won / Lost

My best memory from this game is:

_____

_____

_____

_____

_____

_____

_____

_____

_____

_____

Fan Feedback:

"Come on, two-out rally!"

Tracking my hits

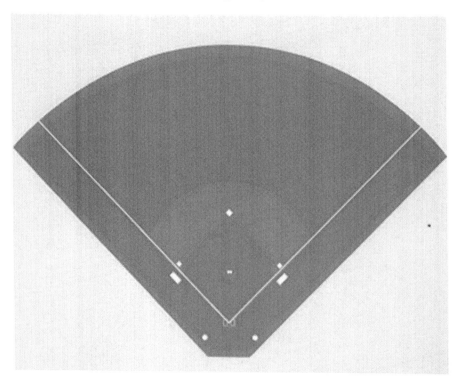

Opponent:

Game Date:

Where:

Positions Played:

Score:

Hitting:

Fielding Errors:

Won / Lost

My best memory from this game is:

_____

_____

_____

_____

_____

_____

_____

_____

_____

Coach's Quote:

"When I say get down, get DOWN!"

Tracking my hits

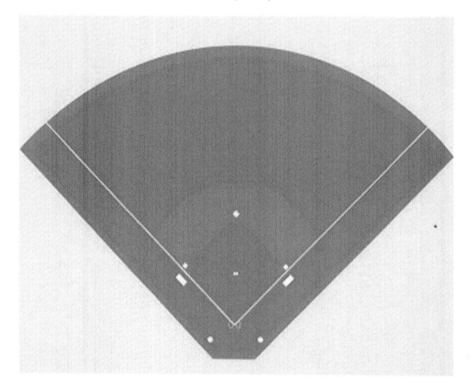

Opponent:

Game Date:

Where:

Positions Played:

Score: Won / Lost

Hitting:

Fielding Errors:

My best memory from this game is:

_____

_____

_____

_____

_____

_____

_____

_____

_____

_____

Fan Feedback:

"Win or lose, YOU had a great game!"

Tracking my hits

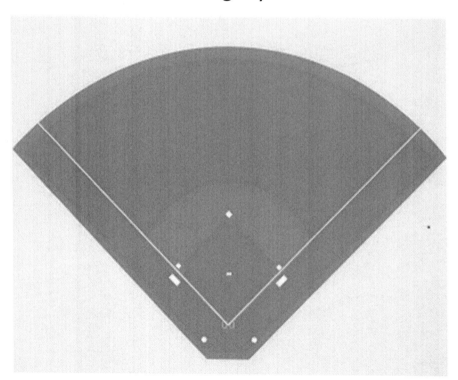

Opponent:

Game Date:

Where:

Positions Played:

Score:

Hitting:

Fielding Errors:

Won / Lost

My best memory from this game is:

Coach's Quote:

"Who's on deck?"

Tracking my hits

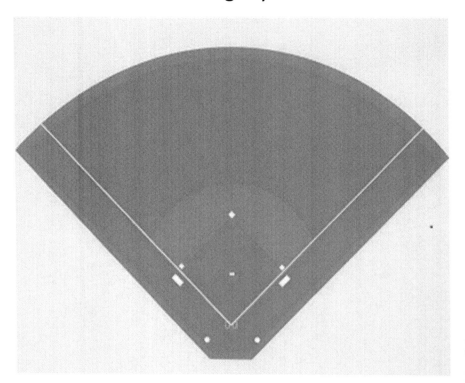

Opponent:

Game Date:

Where:

Positions Played:

Score:

Hitting:

Fielding Errors:

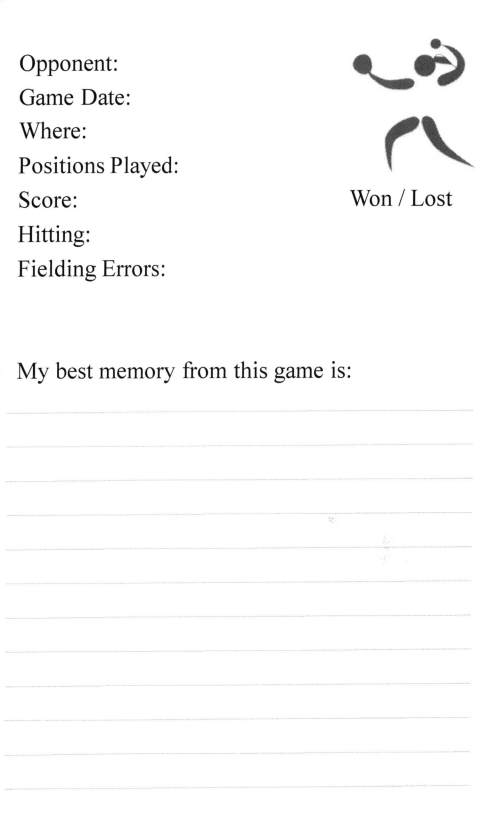

Won / Lost

My best memory from this game is:

Fan Feedback:

"Want a t-shirt?"

Tracking my hits

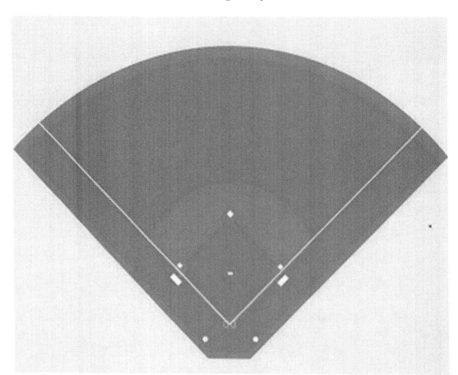

Opponent:

Game Date:

Where:

Positions Played:

Score:

Hitting:

Fielding Errors:

Won / Lost

My best memory from this game is:

_____

_____

_____

_____

_____

_____

_____

_____

_____

Which of these quotes have you heard your COACH say?

Coach's Quotes   X

The most important play is the next one.
Hard work pays off!
Come on, we've gotta have those!
Shake it off!
Somebody make a play!
Know your count!
Get your bat and time her!
New PITCHER!
I can tell who's practicing at home!
Go two, go two!
You've got to hit your cutoff!
I can't want it for you!
Don't watch a third strike!
Be aggressive!
Lay off the junk!
Let's get the bats going!
Great play!
I'll deal with the umpires!
Don't walk on my field!
Have a plan!
Know the situation!
Give her a hard look back, then go ONE!
Did someone get that foul ball?
You've gotta finish your pitch!
Make it a quck half!
Leave it all on the field!
Don't rub it!
What was that?
When I say get down, get DOWN!
Who's on deck?

Which of these quotes have you heard your FANS say?

Fan Feedback	**X**
It's just a game!	
Have fun!	
Keep your eye on the ball!	
Watch the change-up!	
Expect it!	
Did you get a picture of that play?	
Wait on it!	
Field it clean!	
Talk to each other!	
Somebody get an out!	
Don't help her out!	
You're way ahead!	
Good take!	
Not your pitch!	
Watch the ball hit your bat!	
Get dirty!	
Ready position!	
Roll it up!	
Who's idea was it to get white pants?	
Win this game and you can sleep later tomorrow!	
HEADS UP!	
That gate fee is ridiculous!	
Don't tell me I can't bring in my cooler!	
Make sure you're drinking enough water!	
Is all your stuff in your bag?	
Hey, leave those up there!	
We're not playing golf!	
Come on, two-out rally!	
Win or lose, YOU had a GREAT game!	
Want a t-shirt?	

Which states have you traveled to for softball?

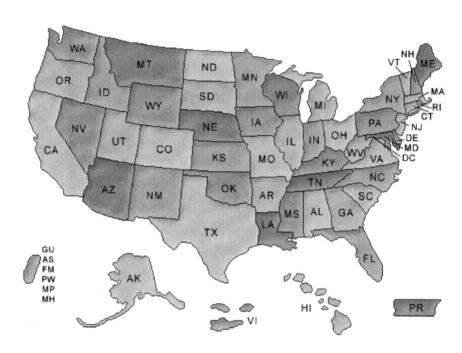

Check out all of our
Ultimate Softball Journals

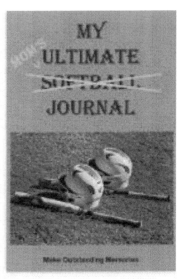

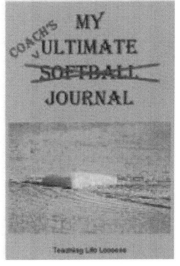

Made in the USA
Middletown, DE
13 December 2017